T0292138

Little Duckie's Day

Story and Pictures by D.L. Skandle

AuthorHouse™
1663 Liberty Drive
Bloomington, IN 47403
www.authorhouse.com
Phone: 833-262-8899

Because of the dynamic nature of the Internet, any web addresses or links contained in this book may have changed since publication and may no longer be valid. The views expressed in this work are solely those of the author and do not necessarily reflect the views of the publisher, and the publisher hereby disclaims any responsibility for them.

This book is printed on acid-free paper.

ISBN: 978-1-4490-9705-9(sc)
ISBN: 978-1-4817-6001-0 (e)

Library of Congress Control Number: 2010908666

Print information available on the last page.

Published by AuthorHouse 02/23/2024

authorHOUSE®

I am a Duckie. I lead a very busy life! I have to take care of myself and my Mommy every day.

This is my
Mommy.
People tell us
we look alike.
Mommy says
they're just
being polite.

I like to start the day by singing.
Good morning, everyone!

Mommy's like me. She likes to
wake up early.

Once we get up, I follow Mommy to the kitchen and tell her all about the dreams I had the night before. She's a really good listener.

In the kitchen,
I wait for
Mommy to
make my
breakfast.

I wait for Mommy to make my breakfast.

BREAKFAST!!!

I like bananas.

After breakfast I help Mommy
do the housework.

We have to make sure
everything is nice and clean.
I clean the coffee table.

I know how important the TV remote is, so I make sure to put it away in a very safe spot.

Once we finish our chores, Mommy and I can go to the park and play.

I like the swings.

And the slide...

And the jungle gym.
Wheeeeeeeee!

After the park, we go back home for lunch. After all that playing in the fresh air, I'm hungry!

When we finish lunch, Mommy and I take a nap. Whew! We did a lot!

After our nap, we're nice and refreshed. I play with my toys while Mommy prepares dinner.

I have to go to her every now
and then and tell her how much
I love her.

Dinner! Mommy cooks my spinach just the way I like it.

I tell her that in my own special way.

Then it's time for my
bath. It's a lot of fun!

Mommy has fun at
bath time, too.

Mommy's very smart. She can read! She reads to me right before I go to bed. I make sure to pay close attention.

Now it's time for bed. I'm so sleepy!

Mommy tucks me in...

… And then goes off to do all the fun grown-up things she does when I'm asleep.

When I grow up,
I want to be just
like Mommy.

Printed in the United States
by Baker & Taylor Publisher Services